D1397277

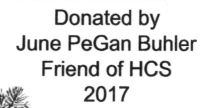

My Day in the
MOUNTAINS

Jory Randall

PowerKiDS press

New York

HUNTINGTON, IN 46750

Published in 2010 by The Rosen Publishing Group, Inc.
29 East 21st Street, New York, NY 10010

First Edition

Editor: Joanne Randolph
Book Design: Julio Gil
Photo Researcher: Jessica Gerweck

Photo Credits: Cover, pp. 9, 11, 13, 19, 21, 23, 24 (top right) Shutterstock.com; p. 5 Philip and Karen Smith/Getty Images; p. 7 Lori Adamski Peek/Getty Images; pp. 15, 24 (bottom left) Rob Gage/Getty Images; pp. 17, 24 (top left) © www.iStockphoto.com/Robert Churchill; p. 24 (bottom right) © www.iStockphoto.com/AVTG.

Library of Congress Cataloging-in-Publication Data

Randall, Jory.
  My day in the mountains / Jory Randall. — 1st ed.
      p. cm. — (A kid's life!)
  Includes index.
  ISBN 978-1-4042-8076-2 (library binding) — ISBN 978-1-4358-2471-3 (pbk.) —
ISBN 978-1-4358-2472-0 (6-pack)
  1. Mountaineering—Juvenile literature. 2. Mountains—Recreational use—Juvenile literature.
I. Title.
  GV200.R36 2010
  796.52'2—dc22
                                    2008051390

Manufactured in the United States of America

Contents

I love climbing to the top of a mountain. I like to look down and see how far we have come.

We start our day in the mountains by walking. Walking up mountain **trails** is called hiking.

Some trails are easy to hike and some are tricky. We hold hands as we cross a fallen tree.

You never know what you might see in the mountains. You might even see a **moose**.

Hiking is hard work. We are ready to stop and have some lunch.

Sometimes we go camping in the mountains. We put up a **tent** and sleep inside sleeping bags.

Camping in the mountains is a lot of fun. We build a **campfire** to cook our food.

I like to fish when I come to the mountains. My dad shows me how to put worms on my hook.

Sometimes we ski when we come to the mountains. Have you ever been skiing?

What a great day we have had in the mountains! I hope we come back soon.

Words to Know

campfire

moose

tent

trails

Index

Web Sites

Due to the changing nature of Internet links, PowerKids Press has developed an online list of Web sites related to the subject of this book. This site is updated regularly. Please use this link to access the list:

www.powerkidslinks.com/kidlife/mountain/

24